Dropping In On...

Washington D.C.

Jeff Barger

Rourke
Educational Media

rourkeeducationalmedia.com

*Scan for Related Titles
and Teacher Resources*

Before Reading:

Building Academic Vocabulary and Background Knowledge

Before reading a book, it is important to tap into what your child or students already know about the topic. This will help them develop their vocabulary, increase their reading comprehension, and make connections across the curriculum.

1. Look at the cover of the book. What will this book be about?
2. What do you already know about the topic?
3. Let's study the Table of Contents. What will you learn about in the book's chapters?
4. What would you like to learn about this topic? Do you think you might learn about it from this book? Why or why not?
5. Use a reading journal to write about your knowledge of this topic. Record what you already know about the topic and what you hope to learn about the topic.
6. Read the book.
7. In your reading journal, record what you learned about the topic and your response to the book.
8. After reading the book complete the activities below.

Content Area Vocabulary
Read the list. What do these words mean?

artifacts
compromise
inauguration
pillars
recreation
solemn
specimens
tomb
tradition

After Reading:

Comprehension and Extension Activity

After reading the book, work on the following questions with your child or students in order to check their level of reading comprehension and content mastery.

1. Why was the site for Washington, D.C., chosen? (Summarize)
2. Why do so many people visit Washington, D.C.? (Infer)
3. Why are the memorials there important? (Asking questions)
4. What memorial or landmark would you most like to visit in Washington, D.C.? (Text to self connection)
5. What is special about the Library of Congress? (Asking questions)

Extension Activity

Create a travel brochure about Washington, D.C. Include several places visitors should see. Write short, exciting paragraphs that highlight the most interesting things about the city. And don't forget to add pictures! You can draw them or print them out from the Internet.

Table of Contents

Washington D.C. Facts

Founded: 1790
Land area: 61.05 square miles (158.12 square kilometers)
Elevation: 150 feet (45.72 meters) above sea level
Previous names: None
Population: 658,893
Average Daytime Temperatures:
winter: 45.7 degrees Fahrenheit (7.3 degrees Celsius)
spring: 66 degrees Fahrenheit (18.7degrees Celsius)
summer: 86.3 degrees Fahrenheit (30 degrees Celsius)
fall: 57.7 degrees Fahrenheit (20 degrees Celsius)

Ethnic diversity:
African-American 49%
American Indian or Alaska Native 0.6%
Asian 4.0%
Native Hawaiian or Pacific Islander 0.2%
Hispanic or Latino 10.4%
White 35.8%

City Nicknames:
The Nation's Capital

Number of Visitors Annually: 20 million

Monumental City

George Washington, the first United States president, picked the location for Washington, D.C., in 1790. His friend, Pierre L'Enfant, designed the city. Pierre wanted the new city to have wide avenues. He lined its streets with trees. He liked open spaces. Great views were his dream. With his design, you can see several monuments from one place.

D.C. Notes
New York was the first U.S. capital, Philadelphia was the second. Washington, D.C., was chosen as the capital in 1791 as a **compromise** with southern states. They thought Philadelphia was too far north.

The National Mall and Memorial Parks manages park properties throughout downtown Washington, D.C., including the Lincoln Memorial Reflecting Pool.

The National Mall is a large area of greenspace that stretches from the U.S. Capitol to the Potomac River. The Mall has some of the most famous monuments in the world. It's like your history book opened and everything jumped out! Do you like fireworks? It's a party on July 4th.

Fireworks light the night sky around the Washington Monument.

Monuments in the National Mall

Monument	Opened
Washington Monument	1888
Lincoln Memorial	1922
D.C. War Memorial	1931
Jefferson Memorial	1943
Vietnam Veterans Memorial	1982
Korean War Veterans Memorial	1995
Franklin Delano Roosevelt Memorial	1997
World War II Memorial	2004
Martin Luther King, Jr. Memorial	2011

Lincoln Memorial
Vietnam Veterans Memorial
World War II Memorial
Washington Monument
Korean War Veterans Memorial
D.C. War Memorial
Potomac River
Martin Luther King, Jr. Memorial
Franklin Delano Roosevelt Memorial
Jefferson Memorial

George Washington
(1732–1799)

Abraham Lincoln
(1809–1865)

An earthquake in 2011 shut down the Washington Monument for nearly three years. The earthquake created 150 cracks in the monument.

At 555 feet (169 meters), the Washington Monument is the tallest building in the city. It is made of marble. An elevator trip to the top takes 70 seconds. The cornerstone was laid in 1848. Abraham Lincoln attended the ceremony. The monument has more than 36,000 stones. It weighs more than 80,000 tons (72,575 metric tons).

The Lincoln Memorial is at the western end of the National Mall. Inside is a 19 foot (5.8 meter) statue of Abraham Lincoln, the 16th president. His Gettysburg Address and Second Inaugural Address are written on the walls of the memorial. The Reflecting Pool starts near the foot of the steps.

Abraham Lincoln became the 16th U.S. president in 1861.

D.C. Notes

President Lincoln was shot in 1865 while watching a play at Ford's Theater near the White House. The building still hosts plays, and has several exhibits and a tour related to Lincoln's death.

The Jefferson Memorial opened during the bicentennial, or 200 year celebration of Thomas Jefferson's birthday. The statue of Jefferson stands at 19 feet (5.8 meters) tall. He faces in the direction of the White House. Surrounding it is an open, marble-domed memorial. It measures 165 feet (50 meters) across.

Thomas Jefferson (1743–1826) was the author of the Declaration of Independence and the third president of the United States.

One of the most popular tourist attractions in Washington, D.C., is the annual blooming of the cherry trees. In 1912, more than 3,000 trees were donated by Japan as a goodwill gesture. You will find these trees next to the Tidal Basin, which is where you also see the Jefferson Memorial.

Citizens of Washington, D.C., who died in World War I (1914-1918) are honored at the D.C. War Memorial. The domed, open building is a memorial and a bandstand. Concerts there are a tribute to those who served.

At the opposite side of the Reflecting Pool is the World War II Memorial. It honors 16 million soldiers who served during that war (1939-1945). Fifty-six **pillars** represent 48 states, seven territories, and one district.

The D.C. War Memorial was designed by three veterans of World War I. It contains the names of the 499 D.C. residents who died serving in World War I.

A field of 4,000 sculpted gold stars on the Freedom Wall of the World War II Memorial commemorate the more than 400,000 Americans who gave their lives during WWII.

Left: The photographs on the Korean War Veterans Memorial were sandblasted into the wall.

Nineteen stainless steel statues stand among bushes. Their ponchos blow in the wind. Granite strips represent neat rows of rice fields. A 164 foot (50 meter) wall contains a mural of more than 2,000 photographs. This is the Korean War (1950-53) Veterans Memorial.

The Vietnam Veterans Memorial is a V-shaped black wall. It holds the names of soldiers who died in the war (1964-1975). Every 10 years, all 58,000 names on the wall are read aloud. It takes several days.

People often bring items such as flags, photographs, and stuffed animals to leave at the Vietnam Veterans Memorial to honor lost family members.

THEY (WHO) SEEK TO ESTABLISH
SYSTEMS OF GOVERNMENT BASED ON
THE REGIMENTATION OF ALL HUMAN
BEINGS BY A HANDFUL OF INDIVIDUAL
RULERS... CALL THIS A NEW ORDER.
IT IS NOT NEW AND IT IS NOT ORDER.

Franklin Delano Roosevelt
(1882–1945)

A statue of a little dog sits next to the president. It is Fala, FDR's beloved Scottish terrier.

Franklin Delano Roosevelt was president for four terms, from 1933 to 1945. Four rooms tell his story at the FDR Memorial. Room one depicts his first **inauguration**. Room two shows a line of statues waiting for bread during the Great Depression. A waterfall crashes over rocks in room three. This represents the beginning of World War II. The last room is The Funeral Cortege.

Out of a mountain of despair, a stone of hope. Those words from Dr. Martin Luther King, Jr. frame his memorial. His 30 foot (9 meter) likeness is carved out of a boulder. Visitors walk past two Mountains of Despair boulders to reach this Stone of Hope. Nearby is a 450 foot (137 meter) wall. It has more than a dozen of Dr. King's quotes inscribed on it.

Dr. Martin Luther King, Jr. (1929–1968)

OUT OF THE MOUNTAIN OF DESPAIR, A STONE OF HOPE

Dr. King's famous "I Have a Dream" speech was attended by an estimated 250,000 people.

Important People, Important Places

The White House is where the president lives and works. It has six floors. Two of the floors are for the president, staff, and family.

So where does the vice president of the United States live? Since 1977, the vice president has lived in a house at the Naval Observatory. It is about 2.6 miles (4.2 kilometers) away from the White House.

The West Wing is where the Oval Office is located and is the primary workplace of the president.

Laws are created by the legislators at the U.S. Capitol. It sits on a hill at the east end of the National Mall. The Capitol is a rotunda, or circular floor plan. It is topped by a dome made of cast iron. On top of the dome is a 19 foot (5.8 meter) bronze statue named Freedom. Members of Congress work in offices connected to the Capitol by subway.

The U.S. Supreme Court used to work in the basement of the U.S. Capitol. Since 1935, it has resided in its own building.

Perhaps the most **solemn** place in America is Arlington National Cemetery. Members of the armed forces and their dependents are buried here. Funerals are held every day except Sunday. It is home to the **Tomb** of the Unknown Soldier. Remains of unknown soldiers are buried in this tomb. Soldiers guard this area every minute, every day of the year.

D.C. Notes
Every funeral is attended by an Arlington Lady. This is a group of volunteers that makes sure that no soldier is buried alone. All branches of the military have a group of Arlington Ladies.

17

Miles of Museums

Nineteen museums are part of the Smithsonian Institution. The largest is the Air and Space Museum. Exhibits inform visitors of the history of flight. Sixty thousand objects are contained in the museum. One of them is the Wright Brothers' plane. You can touch a moon rock here. Spacecraft from moon trips can be explored too.

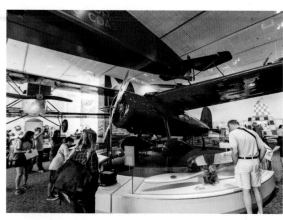

In 1935, Amelia Earhart flew solo from Wheeler Field in Honolulu, Hawaii, to Oakland, California in this plane exhibited at the Air and Space Museum.

D.C. Notes
More than 300 million people have visited the Air and Space Museum since it opened in 1976. A signal from space started a mechanical arm that cut the ribbon for the opening of the museum.

The museum has 21 exhibition galleries.

Animals, plants, and rocks, oh my! The most visited museum in North America is the Natural History Museum. A 14-foot (4.3 meter) tall African elephant greets you on the second floor. You can find living animals in the insect zoo. A real rock star is here too: the Hope Diamond. More than 100 million people have stopped by to see it.

The Hope Diamond was donated to the museum by Harry Winston in 1958.

This once living African elephant has been on display in the museum since 1959.

If history is your favorite subject, the National Museum of American History is like a dream come true. The original Star-Spangled Banner flag is displayed in a two-story case. A top hat from President Lincoln is also on display.

Native Americans are celebrated in the National Museum of the American Indian. One of the museum's highlights is a natural light show. Crystal prisms turn sunlight into rainbow reflections.

This museum is more than a feast for the eyes. During the Living Earth Festival at the Museum of the American Indian, you can sample indigenous foods prepared right before your eyes.

Ginevra is at the Mall, but she's not shopping. She is the only Leonardo da Vinci painting in the Americas. Tourists can see her at the National Gallery of Art. Nearby is the National Portrait Gallery. Portraits of every former president are featured here.

Ginevra's portrait was painted in the 15th century. On the back side of the painting, a wreath of laurel and palm encircles a sprig of juniper with a scroll that bears the Latin inscription, "Beauty Adorns Virtue."

D.C. Notes

On August 24, 1814, British troops set fire to the White House. Dolley Madison, wife of President James Madison, left behind personal belongings and instead saved a portrait of George Washington.

The Holocaust was a mass murder of Jews and other groups during World War II. The United States Holocaust Museum tells the story of this terrible time. Staffers, including Holocaust survivors, help tell the story through the use of **artifacts**. *Remember the Children: Daniel's Story* is an exhibit that explains this time period to young people.

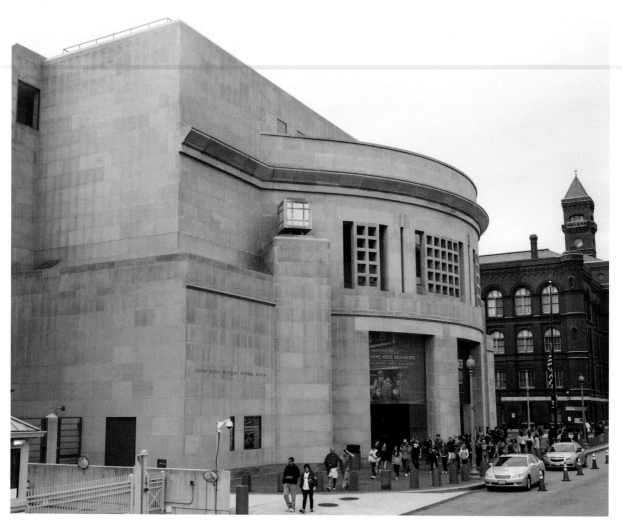

The Holocaust Museum is one of the ten most visited museums in the United States.

The Library of Congress is the nation's library. It not only services members and committees of Congress, but also the executive and judicial branches of government, libraries throughout the nation and the world, and scholars, researchers, artists, and scientists who use its resources.

The Library of Congress is the largest library in the world. It has 838 miles (1,349 kilometers) of bookshelves full of materials. These bookshelves are contained in several buildings. This is an extraordinary amount of books, but they do not have every book published in the United States.

Sports, Food, and Fun

Washington, D.C., isn't all work and no play. There are several professional sports teams in the area.

Citizens' moods rise and fall with the National Football League's Redskins. They've won three Super Bowls to date.

The Nationals of Major League Baseball have a loyal following. The National Basketball Association's Wizards and the National Hockey League's Capitals also call Washington, D.C., home.

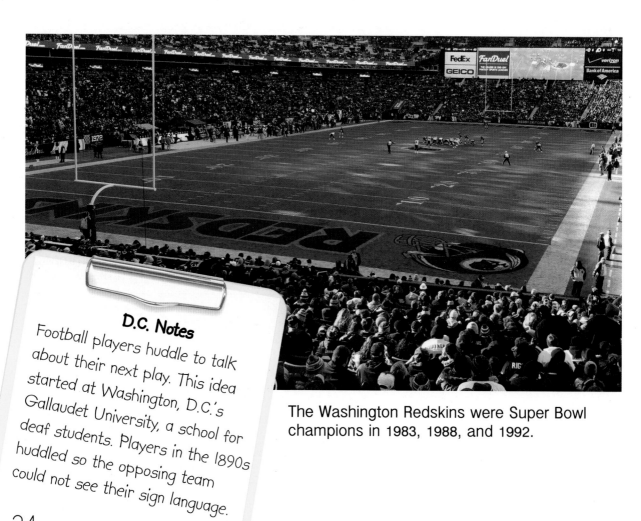

D.C. Notes
Football players huddle to talk about their next play. This idea started at Washington, D.C.'s Gallaudet University, a school for deaf students. Players in the 1890s huddled so the opposing team could not see their sign language.

The Washington Redskins were Super Bowl champions in 1983, 1988, and 1992.

At Rock Creek Park, 32 miles (51.5 kilometers) of trails are available for **recreation**. There's also a horse center, a nature center, and the only planetarium in the national park system.

If you don't like a saddle, try a paddle. Paddle boat, that is! Paddle boat rentals are available near the Jefferson Memorial. You can see the cherry blossoms from the water.

Rock Creek provides excellent opportunities for outdoor activities. The Tidal Basin is a perfect way to get your feet wet on a paddle boat ride.

D.C. Notes

The United States Botanic Garden is near the U.S. Capitol. Thousands of different plant **specimens** reside here. One is the titan arum, or corpse flower. It took nearly ten years for this large plant to bloom. That's good since it gives off a horrible smell!

Walking in D.C., will make you hungry. Where do you go to eat? One unique choice is the Mitsitam Cafe at the National Museum of the American Indian. Diners enjoy native foods from the Americas. The menu is divided into different regions, such as Great Plains and South America.

Region	Food
Northern Woodlands	Smoked Rhubarb Turkey
South America	Crispy Trout with Mango
Northwest Coast	Wild Basil Fried Dough
Mesoamerica	Pulled Chicken, Apricot, and Peanut Mole
Great Plains	Buffalo Burger

MITSITAM MEANS "LET'S EAT!" IN THE PISCATAWAY AND DELAWARE LANGUAGES.

Buffalo burgers are served on buns, just like regular burgers.

Tian Tian and Mei Xiang are on loan to the National Zoo from the government of China.

A 20-minute subway ride from the National Mall will take you to the National Zoo. The stars here are four giant pandas. Other animals include Sumatran tigers, Asian elephants, and cheetahs.

An embassy is a place that represents the interests of a country in a foreign land. In Washington, D.C., several embassies are located on Massachusetts Avenue. During Passport D.C., in May, visitors can tour the different embassies.

In 1878, President Rutherford B. Hayes (1822–1893) invited children for a play date at the White House. That day, the White House Easter Egg Roll **tradition** began. Now, each Monday after Easter, children come to the White House lawn. They roll eggs and participate in other healthy activities. It is the largest event hosted by America's famous home.

The Easter Egg Roll is attended by tens of thousands of people each year.

Timeline

1790
The Residency Act allows the president to select a site for a capital city.

1800
City of Washington becomes the new capital of the United States. The White House is the new residence of the president.

1814
British soldiers invade Washington, D.C., and burn several buildings including the Capitol.

1846
The Smithsonian Institute is started.

1847
The Virginia portion of Washington, D.C., is returned to Virginia.

1865
President Abraham Lincoln is assassinated in Ford's Theater.

1867
African-American males granted the right to vote.

1888
Washington Monument is open to visitors.

1961
Residents of Washington, D.C., receive the right to vote for president.

1963
Martin Luther King, Jr. gives "I Have a Dream" speech.

1981
President Ronald Reagan is nearly assassinated outside a hotel in Washington, D.C.

2001
Terrorists fly a plane into the Pentagon on September 11. Another plane headed for Washington, D.C., crashes in Pennsylvania.

2011
Earthquake centered in Virginia causes cracks in the Washington Monument.

Glossary

artifacts (art-uh-fakts): objects made or changed by human beings

compromise (kom-pruh-mize): to agree to accept something that is not exactly what you wanted

inauguration (in-aw-gyuh-RAY-shuhn): the ceremony of swearing in a public official

pillars (pil-uhrz): columns that support part of a building or that stand alone as a monument

recreation (rek-ree-AY-shuhn): games, sports, and hobbies people enjoy in their spare time

solemn (SOL-uhm): grave or very serious

specimens (SPESS-uh-muhnz): samples, or examples used to stand in for a whole group

tomb (toom): a grave, room, or building for holding a dead body

tradition (truh-DISH-uhn): the handing down of customs, ideas, and beliefs from one generation to the next

Index

Show What You Know

1. What did Dolley Madison save after British troops set fire to the White House?
2. Where does the vice president of the United States live?
3. Who chose the site for Washington, D.C.?
4. Who designed the city?
5. Where can you find the original Star-Spangled Banner?

Websites to Visit

http://washington.org/dc-cool-kids

https://kids.usa.gov

www.si.edu/Kids

About the Author

Jeff Barger is a second grade teacher who lives in North Carolina with his wife and two daughters. He likes dropping in on lots of things including doughnuts, gardens, football games, and libraries.

Meet The Author!
www.meetREMauthors.com

© 2016 Rourke Educational Media

All rights reserved. No part of this book may be reproduced or utilized in any form or by any means, electronic or mechanical including photocopying, recording, or by any information storage and retrieval system without permission in writing from the publisher.

www.rourkeeducationalmedia.com

PHOTO CREDITS: Cover: © Sean Pavone, dibrova, Aleksander Mirksi; Page 1: © Dieter spears; Page 4: © lolie; Page 5: © Red Tack Arts, National Park Service; Page 6: © Luke1138, wynnter; Page 7: ©Tono Balaguer, Scott Smith; Page 8: © Marco Rubino; Page 9: ©Sean Pavone; Page 10: © Zack Frank, James Pruitt; Page 11: © Joel Carillet; Page 12: © Aleksander Mirski; Page 13: © cvandyke; Page 14: © Coast-to-Coast; Page 15: © Pete Souza, nojustice; Page 16: © Wysiati; Page 17: © Aleksander Mirski, Trigger Photo; Page 18: © F11photo, Aoldman; Page 19: © Mbalotia/Wikipedia, Jruffa; Page 20: © Orham Cam, Richard Gunion; Page 21: © Leondardo DaVinci/Wikipedia; Page 22: © Juanmonino; Page 23: © gregobagel; Page 24: © Adam Lubbe; Page 25: © eurobanks; Page 26: © Aleksey Klints; Page 27: © PR NEWSWIRE/AP Images; Page 28: © Kristopffer Tripplaar/Alamy; Page 29: © lolie, Library of Congress, Steve Christensen, nojustice, wynnter, mseidelch

Edited by: Keli Sipperley

Illustrations by: Caroline Romanet

Cover and interior design by: Jen Thomas

Library of Congress PCN Data

Dropping in on Washington D.C./Jeff Barger
ISBN 978-1-68191-405-3 (hard cover)
ISBN 978-1-68191-447-3 (soft cover)
ISBN 978-1-68191-485-5 (e-Book)
Library of Congress Control Number: 2015951571

Printed in the United States of America, North Mankato, Minnesota

Also Available as:

ROURKE'S
e-Books